WHAT IF THERE WERE NO SEA OTTERS?

A Book about the Ocean Ecosystem

by Suzanne Slade

Illustrated by Carol Schwartz

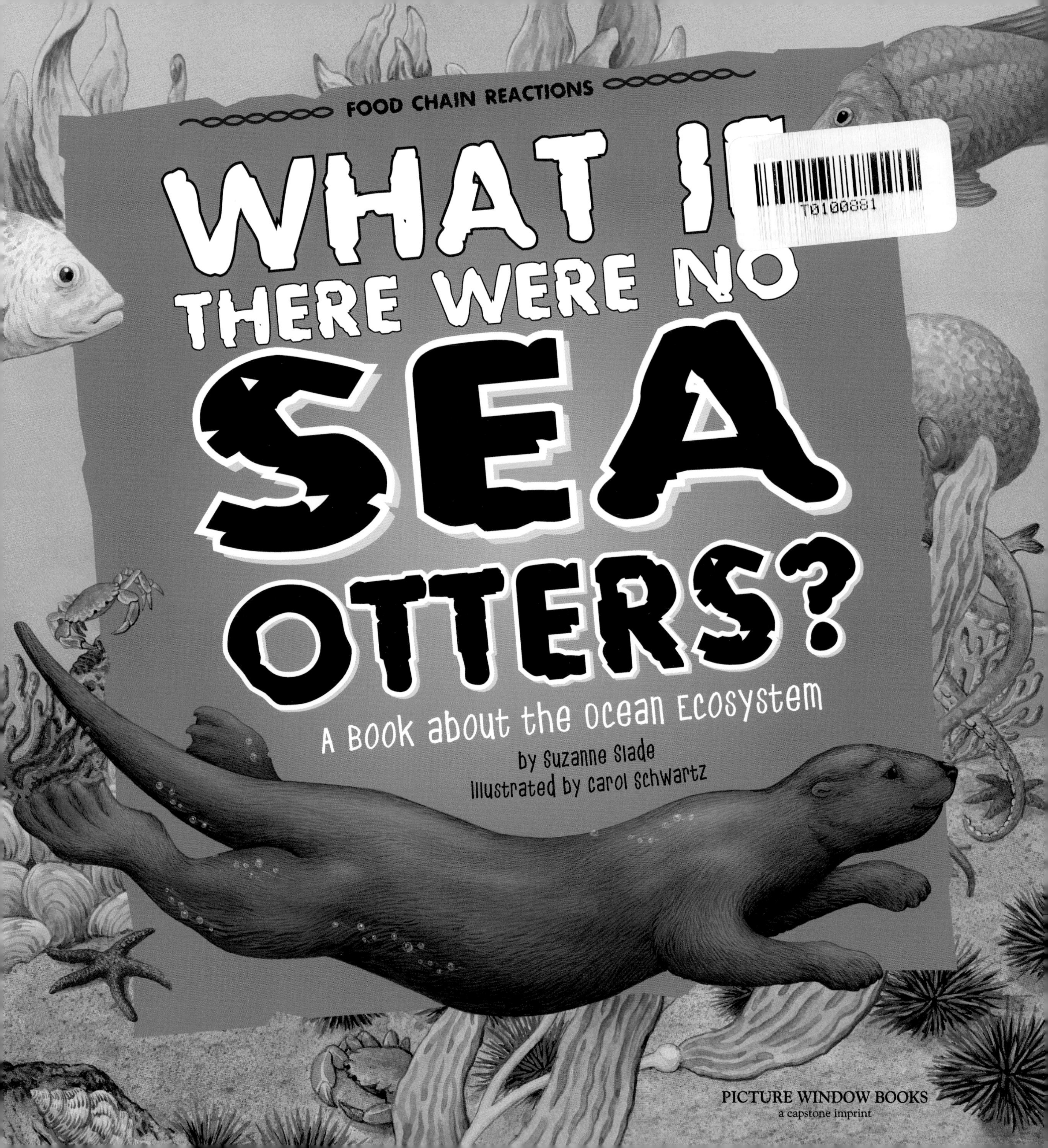

PICTURE WINDOW BOOKS

a capstone imprint

Sea otters know how to have fun. Found in the northern Pacific Ocean, these furry mammals love to tumble and twirl in the water. Sea otters live in kelp forests near the shore, along with colorful fish, crabs, clams, and sea urchins.

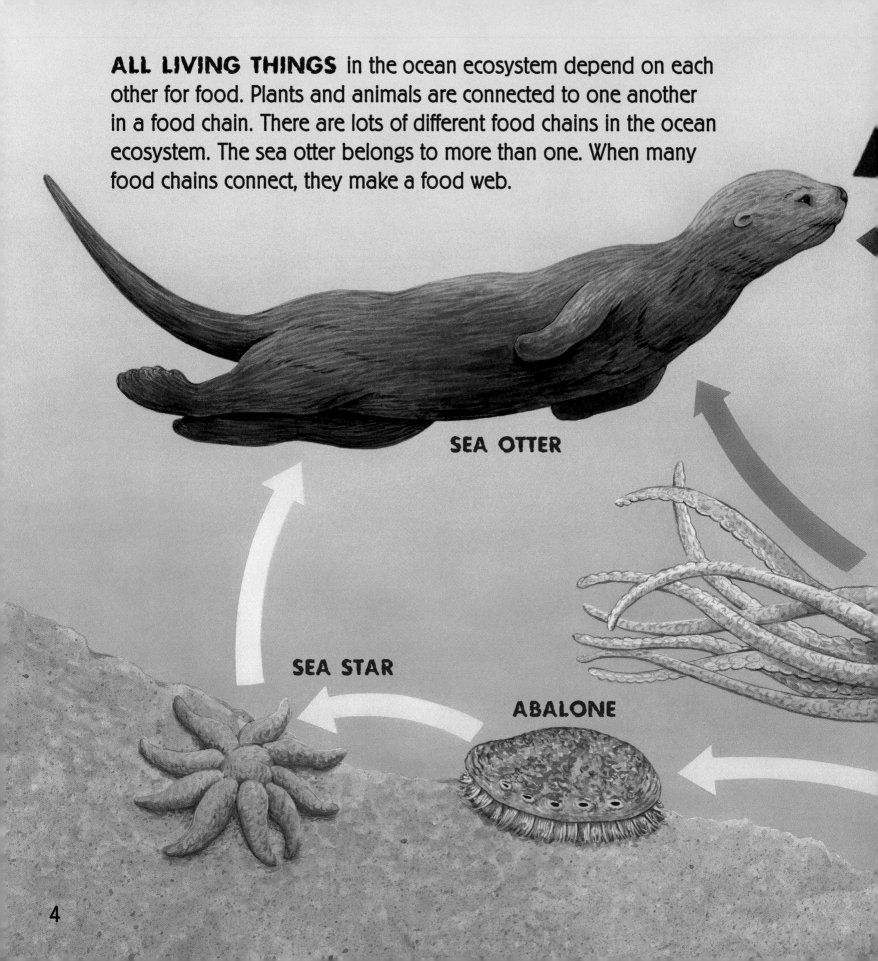

ALL LIVING THINGS in the ocean ecosystem depend on each other for food. Plants and animals are connected to one another in a food chain. There are lots of different food chains in the ocean ecosystem. The sea otter belongs to more than one. When many food chains connect, they make a food web.

SEA OTTER

SEA STAR

ABALONE

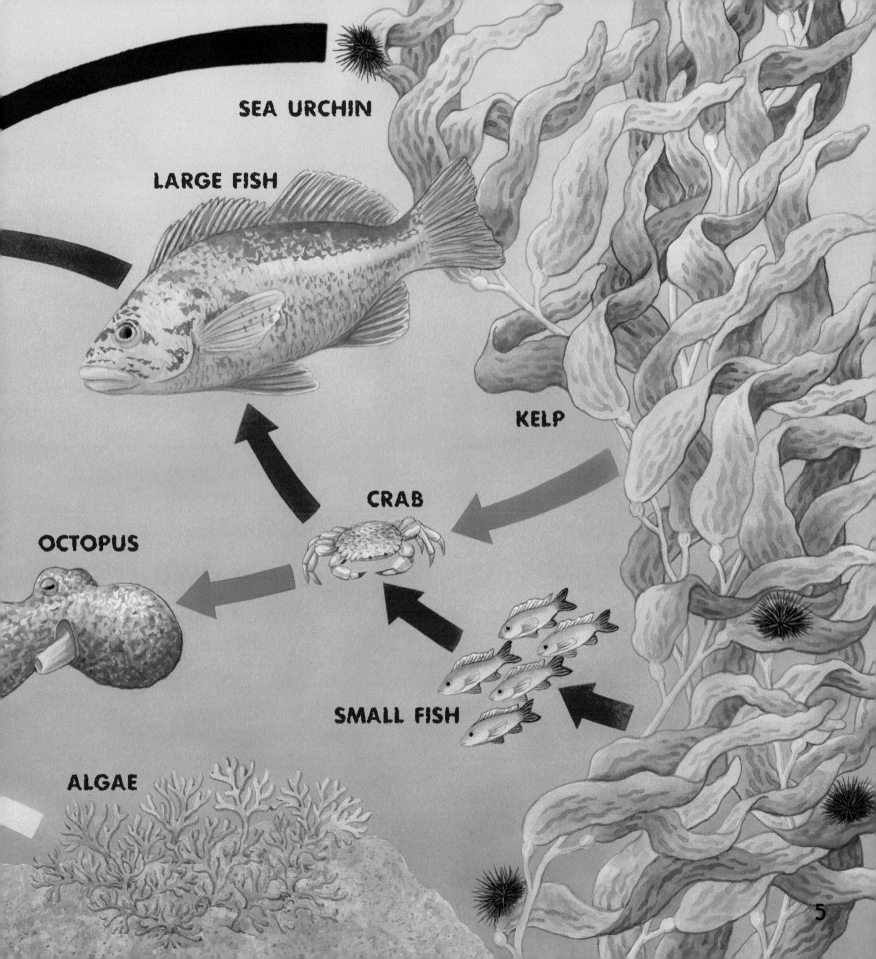

SEA URCHIN

LARGE FISH

KELP

CRAB

OCTOPUS

SMALL FISH

ALGAE

5

SEA OTTERS are big eaters. One adult otter can munch as much as 25 pounds (11.3 kilograms) of food a day. Sea otters enjoy all sorts of tasty treats, including fish, snails, and mussels. But a sea otter's favorite meal is sea urchins.

IT'S CRITICAL

Sea urchins are round, spiny animals. They generally live near the shore, where the water is shallow. Tiny tube feet help them hold on to rocks.

SHARKS AND KILLER WHALES hunt sea otters, but people are the biggest danger. Sea otters get tangled in fishing nets. They're hit by speeding boats. Litter and oil spills turn the animals' watery homes into garbage dumps.

IT'S CRITICAL

A ship called the *Exxon Valdez* spilled 11 tons (10 metric tons) of oil off the coast of Alaska in 1989. The spill killed thousands of sea otters.

As a result, sea otters have already disappeared from some areas. And those areas have changed—for the worse.

WHAT WOULD HAPPEN if sea otters became extinct?

Without hungry otters to dine on them, sea urchin populations would start to grow out of control.

10

IT'S CRITICAL

Sometimes a plant or animal species is so important that without it many other species could become extinct. It's called a keystone species. Sea otters are a keystone species. Keystone species help make sure an ecosystem has many types of life in it.

12

TASTY KELP LEAVES and algae make the perfect meal for sea urchins. But the sea urchins would eat faster than plants could grow. Soon sea urchins would gobble up nearly all plant life near the shore.

IT'S CRITICAL

Kelp is a sea plant that uses sunlight, carbon dioxide, and water to make its own food. All plants do this. The food-making process is called photosynthesis.

SEA URCHINS aren't the only ocean animals that eat plants. Fish, crabs, and snails do too. But before long, they would be in danger. They wouldn't be able to find enough food.

And plants aren't just food. Kelp forests make great hideouts. Small animals hide in the kelp to escape big animals that may eat them. Some fish lay eggs in the kelp and raise their young there. Others use groups of plants as markers to find their way. Without plants, many fish and other small sea animals wouldn't survive.

OCTOPUSES AND SHARKS don't eat plants, but they eat fish and crabs. And fish and crabs rely on plants for survival. If plants disappear, so do large sea animals.

IT'S CRITICAL

Sea stars also eat sea urchins, but they don't eat nearly as many as sea otters do. Sea stars cannot keep the urchin population under control by themselves.

WHAT WAS ONCE a place filled with many kinds of life now looks very different.

NO SEA OTTERS GLIDING THROUGH LEAFY KELP FORESTS.

NO CLUSTERS OF CLAMS ON THE OCEAN FLOOR.

NO CRABS CLICKING THEIR CLAWS.

IT'S CRITICAL

Ocean ecosystems where sea otters have disappeared are called urchin barrens. Barrens are overcrowded with sea urchins and sea stars and have little plant life.

NO GRACEFUL, COLORFUL FISH.

JUST LOTS OF SEA STARS AND HUNGRY SEA URCHINS.

So what would happen if sea otters became extinct? **A LOT!**

One small change, such as the loss of sea otters, can make a big difference in the lives of countless plants and animals. That's why it's so important to take care of our ocean ecosystem.

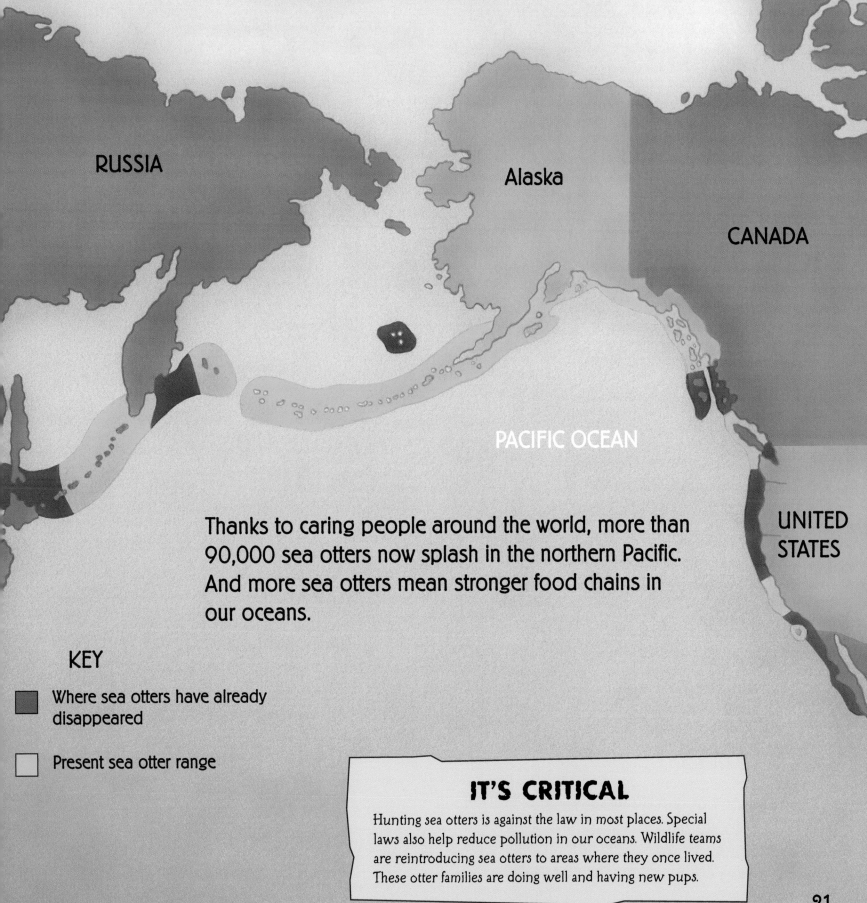

RUSSIA

Alaska

CANADA

PACIFIC OCEAN

UNITED STATES

Thanks to caring people around the world, more than 90,000 sea otters now splash in the northern Pacific. And more sea otters mean stronger food chains in our oceans.

KEY

- Where sea otters have already disappeared

- Present sea otter range

IT'S CRITICAL

Hunting sea otters is against the law in most places. Special laws also help reduce pollution in our oceans. Wildlife teams are reintroducing sea otters to areas where they once lived. These otter families are doing well and having new pups.

OCEAN ANIMALS IN DANGER

The following animal populations are in danger of becoming extinct if nothing is done to protect them:

hawksbill turtle

sawback angelshark

flapper skate

Chinese bahaba fish

Harrison's deepsea dogfish

southern bluefin tuna

hawksbill turtle

HOW TO HELP KEEP OUR OCEANS HEALTHY

- Take shorter showers, and turn off the faucet while you brush your teeth. Saving water helps keep our lakes and oceans cleaner. It also leaves more water for fish and other wild animals and plants.

- Don't litter! Trash can kill all sorts of ocean animals. It can get caught around whales' tails or sea lions' necks. Tiny pieces of plastic may get stuck inside the stomachs of seabirds and turtles.

- Don't pour harmful soaps or chemicals into storm drains. Storm drains lead to canals or rivers. And whatever enters a river will one day reach the ocean.

- Ride your bike or walk instead of taking a car. Cars burn gas, a fuel made from oil. By saving gas, less oil needs be shipped across oceans, reducing the chance of spills.

- Join a wildlife group near you. Groups may have local cleanup days or other events where you can help protect the environment. You can also join a national group, such as the World Wildlife Fund, or raise money to "adopt" an at-risk animal.

Glossary

carbon dioxide—a gas that animals and people breathe out
ecosystem—a group of plants and animals living together, along with the place where they live
extinct—no longer living anywhere on Earth
food chain—a group of living things that are connected because each one eats the other
food web—many food chains connected together
mammal—a warm-blooded animal that feeds its young milk and has fur or hair
reintroduce—to bring back
species—a group of plants or animals that has many things in common

To Learn More

More Books to Read

Fleisher, Paul. *Ocean Food Webs.* Early Bird Food Webs. Minneapolis:
Lerner Publications Co., 2008.

Hooks, Gwendolyn. *Makers and Takers: Studying Food Webs in the Ocean.*
Studying Food Webs. Vero Beach, Fla.: Rourke Pub., 2009.

Lynch, Emma. *Ocean Food Chains.* Chicago: Heinemann Library, 2005.

Internet Sites

FactHound offers a safe, fun way to find Internet sites related to this book.
All of the sites on FactHound have been researched by our staff.

Here's all you do:
Visit *www.facthound.com*
Type in this code: 9781404860186

23

Index

Look for all the books in the Food Chain Reactions series:

What If There Were No Bees? A Book about the Grassland Ecosystem

What If There Were No Gray Wolves? A Book about the Temperate Forest Ecosystem

What If There Were No Lemmings? A Book about the Tundra Ecosystem

What If There Were No Sea Otters? A Book about the Ocean Ecosystem

Special thanks to our advisers for their expertise:
Dana M. Jenski and Suzann G. Speckman, PhD, Marine Mammals Management
U.S. Fish and Wildlife Service, Anchorage, Alaska

Terry Flaherty, PhD, Professor of English, Minnesota State University, Mankato

Picture Window Books
1710 Roe Crest Drive
North Mankato, MN 56003
www.capstonepub.com

Editor: Jill Kalz
Designer: Lori Bye
Art Director: Nathan Gassman
Production Specialist: Jane Klenk
The illustrations in this book were created with traditional illustration, gouache, airbrush, and digitally.

Library of Congress Cataloging-in-Publication Data
Slade, Suzanne.
  What if there were no sea otters? : a book about the ocean ecosystem / by Suzanne Slade ; illustrated by Carol Schwartz.
    p. cm. – (Food chain reactions)
  Includes bibliographical references and index.
  ISBN 978-1-4048-6018-6 (library binding)
  ISBN 978-1-4048-6397-2 (paperback)
  1. Marine ecology–Juvenile literature. 2. Sea otter–Habitat–Juvenile literature. I. Schwartz, Carol, 1954– ill. II. Title.
  QH541.5.S3S54 2011
  577.7–dc22
                2010009879

Printed in the United States   5988